GW01237107

BAUSTELLE BERLIN-MITTE
BUILDING BERLIN

für Helen

Tassilo Bonzel

BAUSTELLE BERLIN-MITTE
BUILDING BERLIN

MICHAEL IMHOF VERLAG

IMPRESSUM | IMPRINT

Tassilo Bonzel: BAUSTELLE BERLIN-MITTE
BUILDING BERLIN

Übersetzung:
Katie Sutton

Layout, Umschlaggestaltung und Reproduktion:
Margarita Licht, Michael Imhof Verlag

Druck:
optimal media GmbH, Röbel/Müritz

© 2020 Michael Imhof Verlag und Tassilo Bonzel

Michael Imhof Verlag GmbH & Co. KG
Stettiner Straße 25, D-36100 Petersberg
Tel. 0661/29191660; Fax 0661/29191669
www.imhof-verlag.de; E-Mail: info@imhof-verlag.de

Printed in Germany

ISBN 978-3-7319-0937-8

INHALT | CONTENT

Vorwort | Preface   10

Diesen Berlin-Trip wirst Du nie vergessen | This is a Berlin Trip You Won't Forget   14

Abbruch des Palasts der Republik | Demolition of the Palace of the Republic   18

Vom Potsdamer Platz nach Unter den Linden | From Potsdamer Platz towards Unter den Linden   20

Über den Bebelplatz | Across Bebel Square   32

Über den Prachtboulevard Unter den Linden | Along the Grand Boulevard Unter den Linden   38

Beim Deutschen Historischen Museum/Zeughaus | At the German Historical Museum in the Arsenal *(Zeughaus)*   48

Über die Schlossbrücke zum Berliner Schloss | Approaching the Berlin Palace across the Palace Bridge   56

Blicke aus der Höhe | The View from above   70

Blick in den Himmel | Looking at the Sky   76

Abstecher zur Baustelle der James-Simon-Galerie | Detour to the Building Site of the James-Simon-Gallery   84

Durch den Lustgarten zum Berliner Schloss | Through the Pleasure Garden to the Berlin Palace   90

Nach Osten um das Berliner Schloss | Eastwards around the Berlin Palace   96

Rund um das Schloss nach Süden und Westen | Around the Palace to the South and to the West   106

Zum Roten Rathaus und weiter zum Werderschen Markt | To the Red Town Hall and on to Werder Market   120

Die U-Bahn U5 wird auch fertig | The underground U5 get's ready, too   134

Erläuterungen | Commentaries   136

Vita | Vita   140

Danksagung | Thanks   140

VORWORT | PREFACE

Die Schönheit Pop-Art-ähnlicher Szenen in Berlin-Mitte: Rot-weiße Absperrungen, goldgelbe Zementcontainer und bunte Wasserrohre kontrastieren mit barocken und klassizistischen Bauten, eine faszinierende Provokation für das Auge und für kulturelles Empfinden. Die Fremdkörper werden umflossen von Autoströmen, Berliner Bürgern und vielsprachigen Touristenscharen, vielleicht mit Assoziationen zum Wirrwarr Babel.

Ich lasse die Großbaustelle in der Mitte, eine der letzten von dieser Bedeutung, am Potsdamer Platz beginnen, sie findet ihren Höhepunkt am Stadtschloss und endet am Roten Rathaus und Werderschen Markt. Die neue U-Bahnlinie U5 spiegelt die städtische Zukunft, im neuen alten Berliner Stadtschloss wird die Vergangenheit für das Humboldt Forum rekonstruiert. Leipziger Platz, Staatsbibliothek ,Haus

Kriegswunden | war wounds | Am Kupfergraben | 2018

The beauty of Pop Art-like scenes in Berlin-Mitte, the historic center of Berlin: red and white street barricades, golden yellow cement containers and colourful water pipes contrast with baroque and classical buildings in a fascinating provocation both for the eye and the viewer's cultural sensibilities. These foreign objects are surrounded by streams of traffic, Berlin residents and multilingual hordes of tourists, evoking associations with the biblical chaos of Babel.

My journey through the massive building site that is in the middle of Berlin, one of the last such significant sites in the city, and situated in the previous socialist "East Berlin", begins at Potsdamer Platz. It finds its climax at the Berlin Stadtschloss (city palace), and ends at the Rotes Rathaus (Red Town Hall) and Werderscher Markt.
The new U-Bahn line U5 reflects the city's future, while in the new old rebuilt Stadtschloss we find the historical past reconstructed to house the Humboldt Forum museum complex. During this single period of construction, sites as diverse as Leipziger Platz, the Staatsbibliothek (national library) at Unter den Linden, the Zeughaus (arsenal), Bebelplatz, and the Neues Museum have all been redeveloped, renovated, transformed, and in some cases, completely reinvented.

All who have found themselves moving through these streets during these many years of reconstruction, walking along the main city axis formed by the famous boulevard Unter den Linden, dodging the barricades, painted fences and pipes, or climbing up to the information centre in the "Humboldt-Box," will have already experienced for themselves this creation of a major new cultural centre, forming their own vivid images. But behind these pictures, behind this actually quite young metropolis, the thoughtful observer also sees multifaceted historical transitions, between Imperial Brandenburg and Prussia, the Weimar Republic, dictatorships, wars, socialism and reunification.

Unter den Linden', Zeughaus, Bebelplatz Berlin, Neues Museum und andere werden im gleichen Baustellenzeitraum entwickelt, renoviert, verändert oder neu erfunden.

Wer auch immer sich viele Jahre lang in den Straßen um die zentrale Achse Unter den Linden durch Absperrungen, bebilderte Zäune und Rohrleitungen bewegte, oder die Humboldt-Box erkletterte, erlebte die Entstehung eines kulturellen Großzentrums in eigenen aufregenden Bildern. Der nachdenkliche Betrachter sieht aber hinter diesen Bildern der eigentlich jungen Großstadt Berlin vielfache historische Wechsel zwischen Brandenburg–Preußen und seiner Monarchie, Weimarer Republik, Diktaturen, Kriegen, Sozialismus und Wiedervereinigung.

Im Bildband „Baustelle Berlin-Mitte" begegnen wir Impressionen aus einer kurzen Epoche, in der die Brüche der Vergangenheit für „ewig" repariert und beendet werden sollen. Dieser kurze Zeitraum zwischen 2007 und 2019 bzw. seit dem Abriss des Palasts der Republik hat mich zu vielen Ausflügen verleitet, dazu, die Veränderungen in zahlreichen Bildern festzuhalten und schließlich mit zunehmender Intensität zur Idee, diese Impressionen in einem Buch zu dokumentieren und zu konzentrieren.
Die fotografische Herausforderung bestand darin, Chaos, Kontraste und Tradition jenseits einfacher Dokumentation unter ästhetisch-künstlerischen Aspekten zu strukturieren.

Nicht-reduzierte Bildsprache und Brüche in der Darstellung spiegeln dabei die heterogene vergängliche Baustellenwelt vor historischem Hintergrund der markanten Baudenkmäler bis zum Ende des 19. Jahrhunderts. Die Spannungen in den Abbildungen entsprechen den Verletzungen der Stadt durch Baustellen ebenso wie den politischen Brüchen.

In this photographic volume, Building Berlin, we are greeted with impressions from a very short epoch, representing attempts to repair and move on "forever" from the ruptures of the past. This short period between 2007 and 2019, starting with the demolition of the Palast der Republik (Palace of the Republic), seat of the former East German parliament, has been my inspiration for many an excursion, as I have worked to capture these changes in a multitude of images. Ultimately, I reached the decision to concentrate and document these impressions in the form of a book.

The key challenge lay in deciding how to bring these images together; how to structure the kaleidoscope of chaos, contrasts and traditions in a way that moved beyond mere documentation to create an aesthetic intervention.

The language of images and ruptures presented here reflects the heterogeneous and temporally constrained world of Berlin building sites, situating these against the historic background of the major building memorials mostly until the end of the 19th century. The tensions in the photographs correspond to the wounds inflicted on the city over the decades, whether in the form of building sites or political ruptures.
But the images today are also full of people, full of stories and therefore full of life. Pedestrians run in front of the camera, cyclists are everywhere, cars force themselves through the bottlenecks of traffic and tourists from everywhere work to create a diverse backdrop. All of these elements may point to an optimistic contemporary society.

Today we live in this country in freedom, and enjoy a level of prosperity that enables us to renovate these sites with the help of modern machinery and clean containers not covered blackened and dirtied, but in beautiful colours, often bathed all together in a warm evening or morning sunlight.

Aber die Bilder sind heute voller Menschen und damit voller Leben und voller Geschichten, Fußgänger rennen vor die Kamera, Radfahrer sind überall, Autos zwängen sich durch Engpässe und Touristen bilden vielfältige Kulissen und spiegeln eine optimistische Gesellschaft.

Ja, wir leben heute in diesem Land in Freiheit und in einer Prosperität, die uns diese Baustelle erlaubt, nicht mit schwarzen und erdverdreckten Geräten, sondern mit sauberen Behältnissen in schönen Farben in meinen Bildern oft getaucht in eine warme Abend- oder Morgensonne.

1963, als ich zum ersten Mal diese Wege ging, war vieles grau, vernagelt oder fehlte und immer war die Staatsmacht der DDR drohend präsent. Jetzt umgibt auch das Chaos der Baustellen die Hoffnung für Frieden in Berlin.

Die Probleme der Zukunft werden andere sein, eine Andeutung könnte die Werbung für digitale Konsumgüter sein: In preußischer Mitte, am zukünftigen Humboldt Forum, geplant auch für außereuropäische Kulturen, sprang uns jahrelang und riesengroß die koreanische Handy-Werbung entgegen, an der zukünftigen barocken Fassade des 18. Jahrhunderts.

Diese Bilder können nie wiederholt werden.

Tassilo Bonzel

Koreanische Werbung am Berliner Schloss | Korean advertisement | 2013 (wie Nr. 82)

When I first passed along these streets in 1963, so much of what I saw was grey, boarded up, or simply missing, and the threatening presence of GDR (East German) state power hovered above the cityscape. In contrast, today's building site chaos contains a certain promise for peace in Berlin.

The problems of the future will be different ones. This is hinted at by an advertisement for digital consumer goods that jumped out at us for many years, right in the middle of old imperial Prussia. On the scaffold of the future Humboldt Forum — intended to house a major centre for the study of non-European cultures, behind a rebuilt baroque 18th-century façade — the passer-by was inevitably struck by an enormous advertisement for Korean mobile phones.

It will never be possible to repeat these images.

DIESEN BERLIN-TRIP WIRST DU NIE VERGESSEN | THIS IS A BERLIN TRIP YOU WON'T FORGET

Ist diese Stadt tot fotografiert? Seit der Erfindung des Mediums Fotografie vor mehr als 180 Jahren steht sie im Fokus von Fotografen, richten diese ihre Kameras auf die Stadt, ihre Bewohner und Besucher. Was Ende des 19. Jahrhunderts mit dem Rollfilm und ersten Handkameras begann, setzt sich heute mit der digitalen Bilderflut fort: das Massenphänomen (Berlin-) Fotografie.

Die Serie „Baustelle Berlin-Mitte" von Tassilo Bonzel weckt – dem Titel nach – die Erwartung einer Dokumentation der baulichen Entwicklung im Zentrum Berlins der letzten Jahre, deren vorläufiger Höhepunkt die Eröffnung des Humboldt Forums ist. Wie erstaunt ist jedoch der Betrachter, da ihn weder eine chronologische Bildfolge von Baufortschritten bis hin zur Fertigstellung beeindruckender Bauten und einladender Stadträume noch klare Gegenüberstellungen von Vorher-Nachher-Bildern erwarten.

Einzig ordnendes Prinzip der Bildfolge ist der Gang des Fotografen zwischen zwei Großbaustellen der Zeit nach 1989: Potsdamer Platz und Humboldt Forum. Beide Orte sind in höchstem Maße historisch „aufgeladen". Ersterer ein Symbol für das Berlin der Goldenen 20er und die deutsche Teilung. Beide stehen für das mehrfache „Überschreiben" von Geschichte durch Aufbau, Zerstörung, Abriss und Aufbau. Dazwischen die barocke Monumentalachse vom Brandenburger Tor zur Spreeinsel zum Herzen der Stadt – ein Touristen-Hotspot.

Die räumliche Kontinuität dieser Strecke wird durch die zeitlich chaotische Anordnung der Bilder und das Zick-Zack der Bewegungen der Kamera mit Abstechern in angrenzende Stadträume aufgebrochen. Hier geht es nicht um das visuelle Erzählen einer linearen Geschichte. Der Fotograf betont das Sprunghafte, die gewaltsamen Brüche der

Has this city been photographed to death? Ever since the invention of the photographic medium more than 180 years ago photographers have had it in their focus, directing their cameras towards the city, its inhabitants and visitors. What began at the end of the 19th century with the first roll films and handheld cameras continues into the present with its flood of digital images: the mass phenomenon of (Berlin in) photography.

The title of Tassilo Bonzel's series "Building Berlin-Mitte" raises the expectation that it will document construction developments in central Berlin in recent years, the provisional climax of which will be the opening of the Humboldt Forum. But the actual images leave the observer startled, providing neither a chronological account of construction progress culminating in the completion of impressive buildings or inviting urban spaces, nor a clear opposition between "before" and "after."

The single ordering principle of this series is the photographer's own passage between two major building sites during the period since 1989: Potsdamer Platz and the Humboldt Forum. Both of these locations are "loaded" with history to the umpteenth degree. The former stands as a symbol for both the Berlin of the "Golden Twenties," as well as the nation's decades of division. Both locations stand for a multilayered "writing over" or "palimpsest" of historical events and narratives, achieved though design and destruction, tearing down and building up again. In between the two stands the monumental baroque axis that runs from the Brandenburg Gate to the Spree Island through the heart of the city – a veritable tourist hotspot.

Diesen Berlin-Trip wirst Du nie vergessen. | This is a Berlin trip you will never forget. | 2018

The spatial continuity of this route is broken up by the temporarily chaotic assembly of the images and the zig-zagging of camera movements that also take detours into neighbouring urban spaces. This is not about visually narrating a linear history. The photographer emphasizes the fissures, the violent breaks in the city's design, the prolonged state of exception and the everyday perception of this state. He delights in unsettling the observer by combining images of the same building in differing formats and from a range of distances, and he surprises them with elements that seemingly reach beyond the individual photograph. He deliberately seeks out perspectives in which the view of the city is obstructed by lampposts and traffic lights, tree trunks, garbage bins, traffic signs, and even people – often out of focus or starkly fragmented. Dominating these disruptive images are temporary architectural forms such as the Humboldt-Box, container fortresses, cranes, and concrete silos, through to lopsided barricades, fences, scaffolding, multicoloured pipes and bizarrely towering iron reinforcements. These enter into an exciting dialogue with the historical monuments, which in turn seem to drown somewhat in the snarl of lines, compartmentalized forms and colours. Frequently, these effects are enhanced by long shadows, for the photographer favours the low angled sunlight of the morning and evening hours.

Bonzel allows us to see a city full of signs and images. Arrows, instructions, signposts and warning symbols barely seem to give any orientation amidst the chaos of the centre – please keep in a line! Multiple layers of stickers and graffiti send cryptic messages. Advertising spaces offer modern flaneurs from all corners of the world promises that at times seem absurd: Marsianer, Unvergleichlich, Reizvolle Touren, Panorama Nights, 100 Jahre Gegenwart, Super (martians, the incomparable, charming tours, panorama nights, 100 years

Stadtgestalt, den andauernden Ausnahmezustand und deren Wahrnehmung im Alltag. Er irritiert lustvoll mit Bildpaaren unterschiedlicher Formate und Distanzen auf gleiche Gebäude, überrascht mit scheinbar bildübergreifenden Elementen. Absichtsvoll sucht er Perspektiven, in denen Laternen- und Ampelmasten, Baumstämme, Mülleimer, Verkehrsschilder, selbst Menschen – oft unscharf und in starkem Anschnitt – den Blick in die Stadt verstellen. In diesen Stör-Bildern dominieren temporäre Architekturen wie die Humboldt-Box, Containerburgen, Kräne, Betonsilos bis hin zu schiefen Absperrungen, Zäunen, Gerüsten, vielfarbigen Rohren und skurril aufragenden Bewehrungseisen. Sie treten in einen spannungsvollen Dialog mit den historischen Monumenten, die in dem Gewirr von Linien, kleinteiligen Formen und Farben zu ertrinken scheinen. Dieser Effekt wird oft durch lange Schatten verstärkt, denn der Fotograf bevorzugt das tief stehende Sonnenlicht der Morgen- oder Abendstunden.

Bonzel lässt uns eine Stadt voller Zeichen und Bilder sehen. Pfeile, Leitlinien, Wegweiser, Warnzeichen geben scheinbar kaum Orientierung im Chaos der Mitte – Bitte einordnen! Mehrfach überlagerte Sticker und Graffiti senden kryptische Botschaften. Werbeflächen bieten den modernen Flaneuren aus aller Welt ihre mitunter absurden Verheißungen: Der Marsianer, Unvergleichlich, Reizvolle Touren, Panorama-Nights, 100 Jahre Gegenwart, Super. Großfotos und -grafiken versprechen ihnen schwebende Leichtigkeit, Hippness, Barrierefreiheit, Vielfalt, Begegnung – „Diesen Berlin-Trip wirst Du nie vergessen."

Die Chaos-Strukturen erscheinen in Tassilo Bonzels Fotografien wie die dynamischen Lebenslinien einer vitalen Stadt, die sich immer wieder neu erfindet. Sie werden zu Sinnbildern für das Schicksal Berlins, „immerfort zu werden und niemals zu sein", wie der vielzitierte Karl Scheffler schon 1910 resümierte.

Das Eingangsbild „Schrott" markiert den Impuls für seine Arbeit. Für einen historischen Moment war die Sicht in den Stadtraum an dieser zentralen Stelle möglich, waren Vergangenheit, Gegenwart und Zukunft in dieses eine Bild zu fassen. Der Blick geht durch die Ruine des Palastes der Republik, einst Sitz der Volkskammer der DDR auf dem Grund des Berliner Stadtschlosses, Richtung Westen zur Friedrichswerderschen Kirche.

Bonzel ist der Stadt seit seinem Studium verbunden. Für das Projekt ist er ein halbes Jahrhundert später immer wieder diese drei, vier Kilometer vom Potsdamer Platz bis zum Roten Rathaus als Berlin-Besucher gegangen oder geradelt – am intensivsten in den Jahren seit Grundsteinlegung des Humboldt Forums 2013.

Kern seines fotografischen Interesses ist nicht die Herstellung repräsentativer Veduten, wie sie seit dem 19. Jahrhundert immer und immer

of the present, fantastic). Billboard photos and graphics promise viewers lightness of being, hipness, mobility, diversity, encounters – this is a Berlin trip you won't forget!

The chaotic structures appear in Tassilo Bonzel's photographs as the dynamic lifelines of a vital city that is always reinventing itself anew. They transform into emblems for the fate of Berlin itself, "always to become and never to be," as the much-cited Karl Scheffler remarked in 1910.

The opening image, "scrap", embodies the key impetus of his work. For a brief historical moment, it was possible to look from this central location into urban space in a way that unified past, present and future. The gaze moves past the ruins of the Palace of the Republic, once the seat of the People's Parliament of the German Democratic Republic, built on the foundation of the Berlin City Palace, and towards the West, to the Friedrichswerder Church.

Bonzel has been connected to the city since his university days. For this project, half a century later, he repeatedly walked or cycled the three or four kilometres from Potsdamer Platz to the Red Town Hall, now as a visitor to Berlin – most intensively during the years since the laying of the foundation stone for the Humboldt Forum in 2013.

At the core of his photographic interest is not the creation of representative large-scale vistas in the fashion of those produced over and over again since the 19th century of that most magisterial of Berlin sights, Unter den Linden. It is barely possible to look at this city without that look also being shaped by the historical photographs in one's head.

Unconcerned and without preconceptions, Bonzel throws himself into the construction site that is the city, perceiving and observing. Working without a tripod and with a digital camera, he is quick and mobile. He intuitively captures the moment in which all of the key image elements are in the right relation to each other, and when the movements of people and traffic create the right combination of colours.

wieder gerade von dieser Magistrale der Sehenswürdigkeiten, Unter den Linden, reproduziert wurden. Es ist kaum möglich, in die Stadt zu schauen, ohne historische Fotografien im Kopf zu haben.

Unbekümmert und ohne Vor-Bilder wirft Bonzel sich in die Baustelle Stadt, diese wahrnehmend, beobachtend. Ohne Stativ und mit digitaler Kamera ist er schnell und beweglich. Intuitiv erfasst er den Augenblick, in dem alle festen Bildelemente in der richtigen Position zueinander und mit Bewegungen von Menschen und Verkehrsmitteln die richtigen Farben beieinander sind. Das Fixieren des Momenthaften, Flüchtigen rückt Bonzel in die Nähe zur Street Photography. Er meidet jedoch Anekdotisches wie komische Szenen, verliebte Blicke, Gesichter in Großaufnahmen oder Kaffeehaus-Beobachtungen.

Menschen zeigt er meist in Bewegung: als aneinander vorbei eilende Passantenmassen, Touristen-Gruppen, Familien, Paare oder Einzelne – die Straße querend, Autos ausweichend, schauend, fotografierend, sich einen Weg bahnend. Sie wirken eilig, erschöpft, auch entspannt, mitunter verloren und bedroht vom Getriebe der Transformation. „... dann zeigt die Stadt dir asphaltglatt im Menschentrichter Millionen Gesichter", schrieb Kurt Tucholsky 1930.

In zwei Intermezzi reißt uns der Fotograf wie ein Regisseur aus diesem Menschen- und Bilderstrom: einige Blicke in den Himmel, grafisch, fast abstrakt, und Übersichten von erhöhter Position bis zum Horizont. Letztere erlauben die Einordnung seiner farbenreichen Impressionen in den Stadtzusammenhang, bevor wir mit Bonzel wieder eintauchen in die allumfassende Bewegung.

Seit mehr als 10 Jahren verfolgt Tassilo Bonzel in eigenem Auftrag Foto-Projekte, in denen er lebendige Situationen und Bilder einfängt, die ein Gefühl für den Charakter von Städten verschiedener Kontinente vermitteln. Er wechselt dabei Stilmittel und Perspektiven. Mit „Baustelle Berlin-Mitte" fügt Bonzel der Fülle der Berlin-Bilder eine sehr eigene, bewusst persönliche Sicht hinzu. Ein Beitrag zum neuen Berlin.

Ines Hahn

Pinning down the transitory moment, Bonzel's work moves in the vicinity of street photography. Yet he avoids the anecdotal – humorous scenes, smitten looks, close-ups of faces or coffee house observations.

He sees people first and foremost in a state of movement – as masses of pedestrians passing each other by in a rush, tourist groups, families, couples or individuals – crossing the street, steering clear of cars, looking, photographing, making a path for themselves. They appear hurried, exhausted, but also relaxed, and sometimes lost or threatened by the bustle of transformation; "...then the city shows you millions of faces, asphalt-smooth, in the sinkhole of humanity," wrote Kurt Tucholsky in 1930.

In two intermezzi the photographer rips us out of the current of people and images like a director: gazing into the sky, graphic, almost abstract, and in synoptic views from above that reach to the horizon. The latter allow for an ordering of his richly coloured impressions into the connectedness of the city, before we dive, together with Bonzel, back into the all-encompassing movement.

For more than 10 years Tassilo Bonzel has pursued photographic projects of his own volition, capturing animated situations and images that communicate a sense of the character of the cities of various continents. In doing so he switches between stylistic devices and perspectives. With "Building Berlin-Mitte" Bonzel adds to the abundance of Berlin images a decidedly unique and consciously personal point of view. A contribution to the new Berlin.

ABBRUCH DES PALASTS DER
REPUBLIK | DEMOLITION OF THE PALACE OF
THE REPUBLIC

Schrott | scrap metal | 2007*

VOM POTSDAMER PLATZ | FROM POTSDAMER PLATZ TOWARDS
NACH UNTER DEN LINDEN | UNTER DEN LINDEN

Häuserabbruch | demolition of houses | 2016

Wasserrohre über dem Potsdamer ... | waterpipes above Potsdamer ...

... und Leipziger Platz | ... and Leipziger Platz | 2013 *

Bauschutt | building debris | 2011

letzte Baulücke am Leipziger Platz | the last building gap at Leipziger Platz | 2018

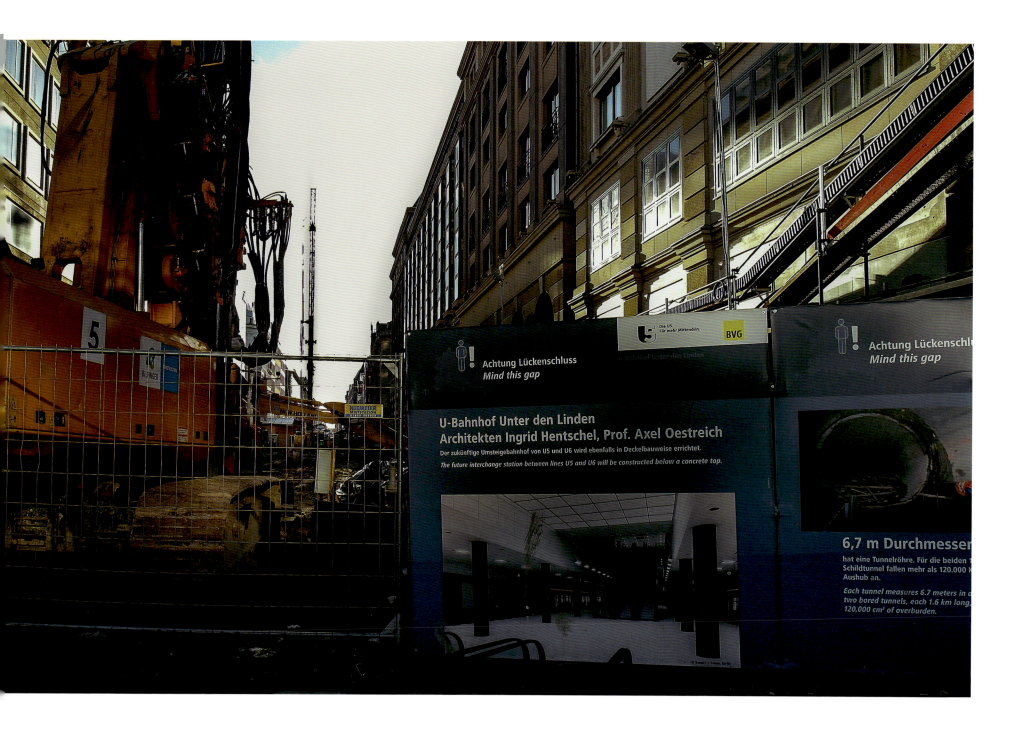

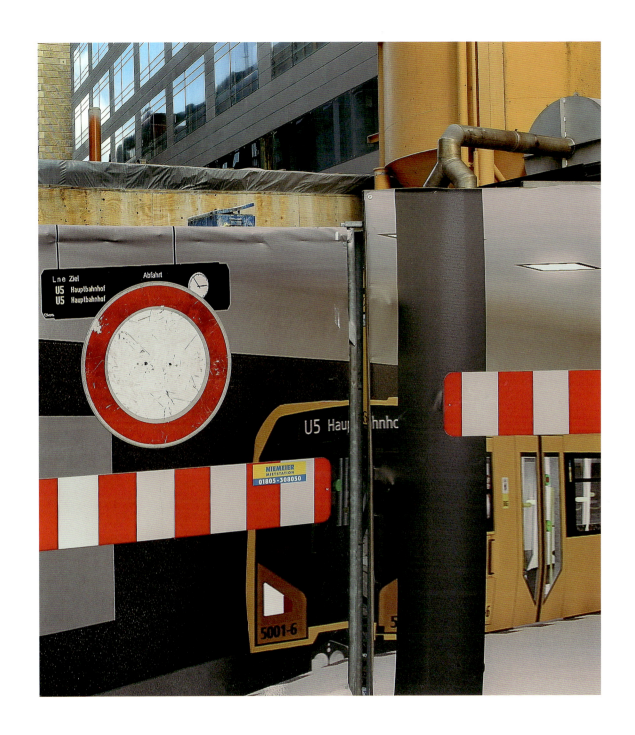

... U5-Bauzaun | ... the fencing around the U5 underground railway site | 2012*

politisches Plakat Unter den Linden | political billboard Unter den Linden, 2013 | 2013*

Blick in die Behrenstraße | the view into Behrenstaße | 2014

Gerüste an der Staatsbibliothek | scaffolding at the National Library | 2014

ÜBER DEN BEBELPLATZ | ACROSS BEBEL SQUARE

Staatsoper | National Opera | 2014*

33

Besucher am Mahnmal der Bücherverbrennung | visitors at the memorial 'Library of Burned Books' | 2014*

St. Hedwigs-Kathedrale | St. Hedwig's Cathedral (Catholic) | 2016

▼ Blick über den Bebelplatz zur Humboldt-Universität | the view across Bebel Square towards Humboldt-University | 2018

ÜBER DEN PRACHTBOULEVARD | ALONG THE GRAND BOULEVARD
UNTER DEN LINDEN | UNTER DEN LINDEN

im Abendlicht | in the evening light | 2015*

Touristen | tourists | 2015

→ Gendarmenmarkt   400m
→ St. Hedwigs Kathedrale   150m
→ Denkmal zur Erinnerung an die 100m
   Bücherverbrennung

Zementsilo und ... | cement silo and ... | 2013 ...

... Tetra Pak-Bauzaun | ... Tetra Pak site hoarding | 2012*

BEIM DEUTSCHEN HISTORISCHEN MUSEUM/ZEUGHAUS | AT THE GERMAN HISTORICAL MUSEUM IN THE ARSENAL *(ZEUGHAUS)*

kein Zugang durch das Drehkreuz | no access through revolving gate | 2018

Bauzaun U5 | U5 building site hoarding | 2019

Unter den Linden voll gesperrt | total barricade of Unter den Linden | 2019

Fertig: frisch gestrichen | finished: freshly painted | 2019

ÜBER DIE SCHLOSSBRÜCKE | APPROACHING THE BERLIN PALACE
ZUM BERLINER SCHLOSS | ACROSS THE PALACE BRIDGE

in der Mitte des Chaos mit Humboldt-Box | in the middle of chaos with Humboldt-Box | 2015*

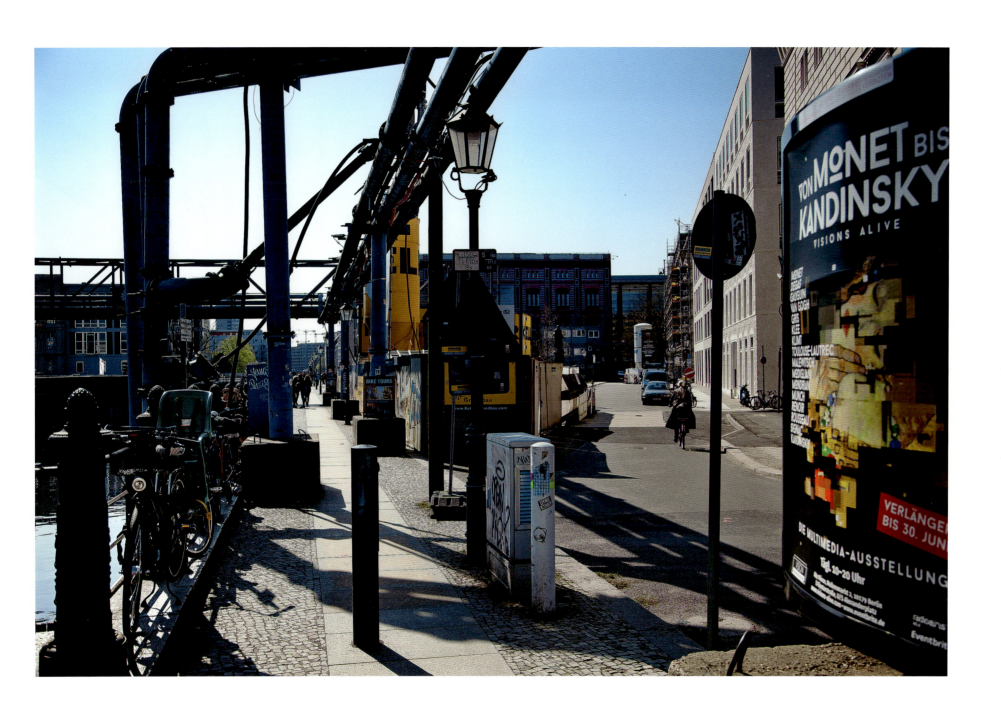

zum Schinkelplatz | towards Schinkel Square | 2018

Kronprinzenpalais | Crown Prince's Palace | 2018

endlich das Schloss! | at last the Palace! | 2016

Neujahrslauf | New Year's run | 2019

abgesperrt | blocked | 2017

Blick über die Schlossbrücke ... | the view across the Palace Bridge ... | 2015

... von der Alten Kommandantur (rechts) | ... from the Alte Kommandantur (on the right) | 2018

Berliner Dom und Humboldt-Box | Berlin Cathedral and Humboldt-Box | 2012

am Kupfergraben | at the Kupfergraben canal | 2012

Schloss im Abendlicht | evening light on the palace | 2015   blaue Humboldt-Box | blue Humboldt-Box | 2018

BLICKE AUS DER HÖHE | THE VIEW FROM ABOVE

Blick über den leeren Schlossplatz | the view across the vacant Palace Square | 2012*

U5-Station Museumsinsel | U5 station Museumsinsel | 2016

Ostfassade des Humboldt Forums | eastern façade of the Humboldt Forum | 2016

... und zum Brandenburger Tor | ... and Brandenburger Tor | 2016

BLICK IN DEN HIMMEL | LOOKING AT THE SKY

griechische Siegesgöttin Nike | the greek goddess of victory Nike | 2015*

Friedrich der Große Unter den Linden | equestrian statue of King Friedrich II of Prussia | 2016

Schlosskuppel | palace dome | 2016

Äste und Streben | branches and struts | 2015   das Treffen der Baukräne | get together of building cranes | 2013

ABSTECHER ZUR BAUSTELLE | DETOUR TO THE BUILDING SITE
DER JAMES-SIMON-GALERIE | OF THE JAMES-SIMON-GALLERY

Bauplatz vor dem Neuen Museum | building site in front of the Neues Museum | 2012

Blick vom Lustgarten ... | the view from the Pleasure Garden ... 2017

... auf das Bauschild | ... onto the construction sign board | 2018

Blick über die Schlossbrücke mit Pallas Athene | the view across the Palace Bridge and Pallas Athena | 2018

DURCH DEN LUSTGARTEN | THROUGH THE PLEASURE GARDEN
ZUM BERLINER SCHLOSS | TO THE BERLIN PALACE

▲ Septembertag im Lustgarten | September day in the Pleasure garden | 2016   Fassaden rot und mit Bus ... | façades red and with bus ...

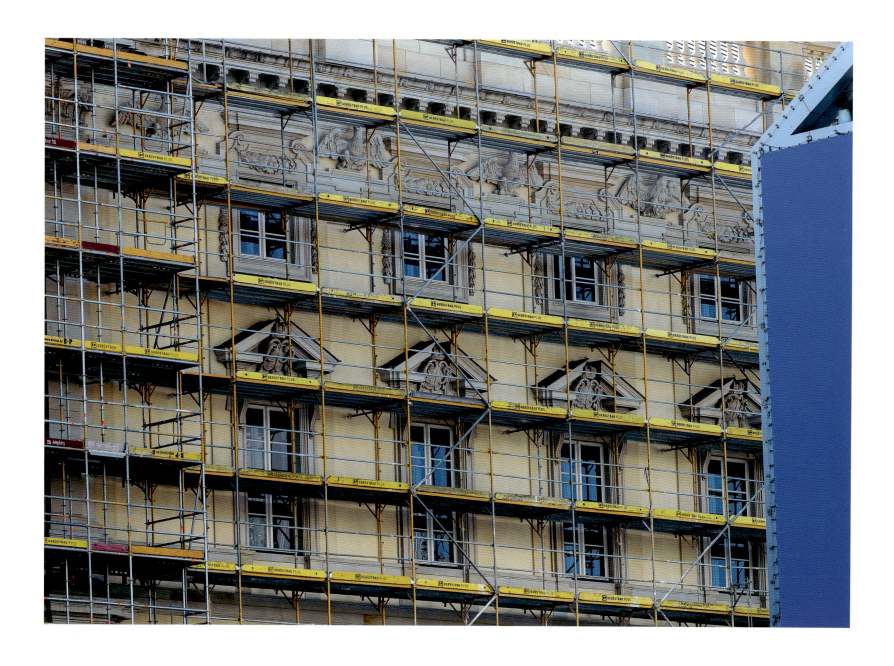

Fassade blau … | blue façade …

NACH OSTEN | EASTWARDS AROUND
UM DAS BERLINER SCHLOSS | THE BERLIN PALACE

Blick nach Westen | the westward view | 2015

Friedrich Engels und Karl Marx blicken auf die Ostseite | Friedrich Engels and Karl Marx look at the eastern façade | 2018

grüne und blaue … | green and blue…

... und rote Rohre | ... and pink pipes | 2015

Der Baubeginn an der Ostseite über der Spree ... | the start of the construction ... | 2013

... und spätere Ostfassade des Humboldt Forums | ... and the façade of the future Humbolt Forum above the Spree river | 2018

Blick über die Spree zur Südfassade ... | view across the Spree towards the southern façade ... | 2018

... und zum fertigen Südostflügel | ... and the completed south-east wing | 2019

RUND UM DAS SCHLOSS
NACH SÜDEN UND WESTEN

AROUND THE PALACE TO THE
SOUTH AND TO THE WEST

temporäre Kunsthalle Berlin nach Abriss des Palasts der Republik | temporary Art Hall Berlin after demolition of the Palace of the Republic | 2009*

Stahlreste vor dem Berliner Dom | steel remnants in front of the Berlin Cathedral | 2009

Schlossaufbau hinter dem Zaun | Palace reconstruction behind fence | 2009

südliche Baustelleneinfahrt ... | southern construction site entrance ... | 2013

... und spätere Südfassade | ... and later southern façade | 2018

fast fertig: Südseite... | nearly finished: southern façade | 2018

...und Südwestflügel | ...and south-west wing | 2018

Westfassade mit Kuppel... | western façade with dome... | 2015

...und Eosanderportal | ...and Eosander Gate | 2018

ZUM ROTEN RATHAUS UND WEITER | TO THE RED TOWN HALL AND ON TO
ZUM WERDERSCHEN MARKT | WERDER MARKET

Rotes Rathaus | Red Town Hall | 2015

U5-Baustelle am Roten Rathaus |
U5 construction site at Red Town Hall | 2013

Baustelle U5 mit Humboldt-Box | U5 construction site with Humboldt-Box | 2015

Baustelle U5 mit Dom | U5 construction site with Cathedral | 2013

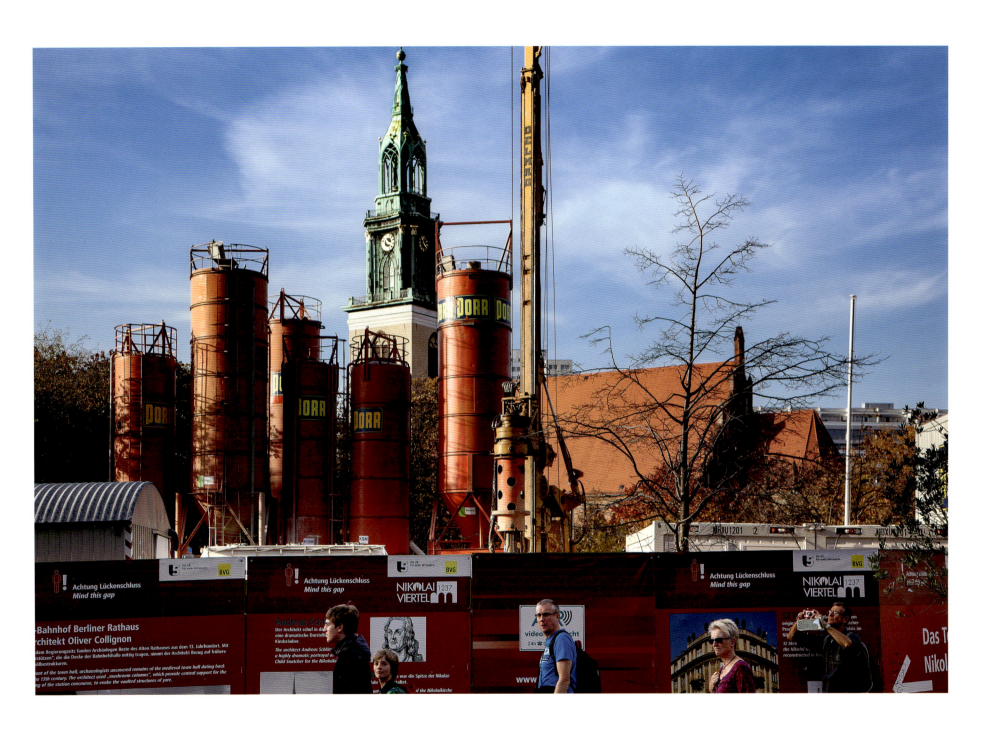

St. Marienkirche | St. Mary's Church | 2015

Baucontainer | construction container | 2015

Containerstapel | container stack | 2015

... und vor dem Neubau mit Dom | ... and before the new building with cathedral ... | 2013*

DIE U-BAHN U5 | THE UNDERGROUND U5
WIRD AUCH FERTIG | GET'S READY, TOO

Eingang zur U5-Station Brandenburger Tor | entrance to the U5 Station Brandenburger Tor | 2019

ERLÄUTERUNGEN | COMMENTARIES

Einige historische Zahlen zu Berlin:

Die Barockisierung des Berliner Stadtschlosses erfolgte um 1700 und die barocken Fassaden waren jetzt Ziel des Wiederaufbaus. Die erste U-Bahn wurde 1902 eröffnet. Das Königreich Preußen dauerte von 1701 bis 1918, in 1871 wird der preußische König Deutscher Kaiser; 1. Weltkrieg von 1914 bis 1918, Weimarer Republik bis zur nationalsozialistischen Diktatur 1933. Im 2. Weltkrieg wurde Berlin weitgehend zerstört, danach aufgeteilt in Westberlin unter Kontrolle der alliierten Westmächte und in Ostberlin unter sowjetischer Herrschaft und Kontrolle der Deutschen Demokratischen Republik (DDR). 1989, vor 30 Jahren, wurde Deutschland wiedervereinigt und in Berlin begann eine Phase umfassenden (nachgeholten) Wiederaufbaus, Umbaus und Neubaus.

S. 19

Das im 2. Weltkrieg ausgebrannte barocke Berliner Stadtschloss wurde 1950 auf Beschluss der SED (Sozialistische Enheitspartei Deutschlands) gesprengt. An gleicher Stelle wurde 1973 der Palast der Republik als Sitz der Volkskammer der DDR errichtet. Nach der Wiedervereinigung wurde der Palast 2006 abgerissen, um das alte Berliner Stadtschloss (modifiziert) wieder aufzubauen.

S. 26/27

Die neu zu bauende U-Bahnlinie U5 überschreitet die alte Grenze zwischen West- und Ostberlin und verbindet den neuen Hauptbahnhof und das Regierungsviertel mit der bereits bestehenden nach Osten führenden U5-Linie am Alexanderplatz.

A few historical facts about Berlin:

About 1700 the Berlin City Palace was renovated in the baroque style, which is now in part restored. The first underground line was opened in 1902. The Kingdom of Prussia existed from 1701 until 1918, from 1871 the King was also the German Emperor. World War I dominated the years 1914 through 1918, followed by the democratic Weimar Republic, which was terminated by the National Socialist (Nazi) dictatorship in 1933. Devastation of Berlin during World War II, then division of the city into West Berlin under Allied Control and East Berlin under the control of the Soviets and the German Democratic Republic (GDR). In 1989, 30 years ago, Germany and Berlin were reunited. This was the start of a period of widespread (late) reconstruction, building, and renovation.

p. 19

The baroque Berlin Palace was burnt out during World War II and the ruins were blown up following a decision by the East German SED (Socialist Unity Party of Germany) in 1950. The Palace of the Republic was built on the same ground, housing the People's Parliament of the GDR (German Democratic Republic). After German reunification, the Palace of the Republic was demolished in 2006 to reconstruct a modified version of the historical baroque palace.

p. 26/27

The new underground line U5, pictured under construction, crosses the previous border from west to east and connects the new main station and government district with the preexisting eastbound underground line at Alexanderplatz, one of the major city squares.

S. 28
Auf dem Plakat von 2013 sind die Spitzen der Großen Koalition bis 1969 zu sehen: Kurt Georg Kiesinger, CDU (2.v.l., Kanzler), Franz-Josef Strauss, CSU (Finanzminister), und Willi Brandt, SPD (Vizekanzler), sowie Gerhard Stoltenberg (2.v.r. Verteidigungsminister).

p. 28
The politicians on the 2013 billboard formed the head of the German government until 1969, including Kurt Georg Kiesinger, CDU (2nd from left, Chancellor), Franz-Josef Strauss, CSU (Treasury Secretary), and Willi Brandt, SPD (Vice-Chancellor).

S. 22 ff
Über die Rohre wird Grundwasser aus Baugruben abgepumpt. Die geschlossene Bebauung des achteckigen Leipziger Platzes wurde in mehreren Teilstücken wiederhergestellt, die letzte Lücke wird 2020 geschlossen sein.

p. 22 et seqq.
Through huge pipes the groundwater drained out of the excavations is pumped into the nearby river Spree. The reconstruction of the building sections at the octagonal Leipziger Platz, destroyed during and after World War II, has been completed in several stages and will be finalized in 2020.

S. 32
August Bebel war einer der Mitbegründer der Deutschen Sozialdemokratie im 19. Jahrhundert im Kaiserreich.

p. 32
August Bebel was a co-founder of German social democracy in the 19th century during the German Imperial period.

S. 33
Die Staatsoper Unter den Linden wurde nach Generalsanierung am 31. August 2019 wiedereröffnet.

p. 33
The National Opera at Unter den Linden was reopened on August 31, 2019, following a complete renovation.

S. 34
Die ‚Versunkene Bibliothek' von Micha Ullmann erinnert mit einem unterirdischen Denkmal an die Bücherverbrennung durch die Nationalsozialisten, die am 10. Mai 1933 hier einen Höhepunkt hatte. Durch eine gläserne Bodenplatte in Platzmitte blickt man in einen unterirdischen Raum mit leeren Betonregalen für 20.000 verbrannte Bücher.

p. 34
The 'Library of Burned Books' is an underground memorial, which reminds us of the Nazi book burning on Mai 10, 1933. Through a glass plate set in the paving stones, visitors can look down into empty bookshelves with space for 20,000 burnt books.

S. 39 und 44
Der Boulevard Unter den Linden mit den Großbaustellen der U-Bahn-linie 5 (U5) und des Stadtschlosses. V. l. n. r. Deutsches Historisches Museum im alten Zeughaus, Turm des Roten Rathauses, Humboldt-Box, Neubau des Berliner Schlosses, Alte Kommandantur, Kronprin-zenpalais, auf S. 44: rechts Staatsoper.

S. 46 und 47
Die Verpackungsfirma ‚Tetra Pak' wirbt an diesem Bauzaun für die ‚Clean Tech Media Awards', die das Unternehmen gesponsert hat (Dr. Heike Schiffler, Tetra Pak).

S. 57
Die Humboldt-Box auf dem Schlossplatz war von 2011 bis Ende 2018 Ausstellungs- und Informationsgebäude, oben mit Besucherterrassen. Die Außenflächen wurden mehrfach für Werbung in verschiedenen Farben verändert.

S. 71
V.l.n.r. Berliner Dom, Turm der St. Marienkirche, Berliner Fernsehturm, Riesenrad, Rotes Rathaus, rechts vorne der leere Schlossplatz nach Abriss des Palasts der Republik.

S. 77
Nike, die Siegesgöttin aus der griechischen Mythologie, erscheint mehrfach als Pfeilerstatue auf der Berliner Schlossbrücke und erlaubt Assoziationen zur Berliner Geschichte, zur Siegessäule oder leichter zum Sportartikelhersteller ‚Nike'.

p. 39 und 44
The images depict the Boulevard Unter den Linden with the large building sites of the underground line U5 and Berlin Palace. From left to right: German Historical Museum in the old Arsenal, tower of the Red Town Hall, Humboldt-Box, reconstruction of the Berlin Palace, Alte Kommandantur (former military headquarters), Crown Prince's Palace; page 44 on the right: National Opera.

p. 46 und 47
The packaging company 'Tetra Pak' advertises on the building fence for the 'Clean Tech Media Awards', which were sponsored by the company (Dr. Heike Schiffler, Tetra Pak).

p. 57
The Humboldt-Box, located on the Palace Square from 2011 until the end of 2018, served as an information and expo building, complete with a visitors' terrace. For advertising purposes, the outside colors were changed several times.

p. 71
From left to right: Berlin Cathedral, tower of St. Mary's, Berlin Television Tower, ferris wheel, Red Town Hall, and the empty Palace Square after demolition of the Palace of the Republic (front right).

p. 77
Nike, the goddess of victory from Greek mythology, appears several times as a pillar statue on the Berlin Palace Bridge, lending associations both to the history of Berlin, especially the Siegessäule (Berlin Victory Column), or more readily, to the famous sporting goods manufacturer

S. 89
Die James-Simon-Galerie (Simon war wilhelminischer Kunstmäzen), erbaut vom Architekturbüro David Chipperfield, wurde am 12.7. 2019 zur äußeren Vollendung der Museumsinsel eröffnet.

S. 107
Die privat finanzierte temporäre Kunsthalle bestand von September 2008 bis August 2010 und war Produktionsort und Schaufenster für die bedeutende internationale Gegenwartskunst in Berlin.

S. 118
Auf dem mittleren Sockel steht der preußische Baumeister Karl Friedrich Schinkel, Gründer der durch Bomben zerstörten Schinkelschen Bauakademie, die dahinter als Attrappe zu sehen ist, aber wieder aufgebaut werden soll.

S. 133
V.l.n.r. Friedrichswerdersche Kirche, Berliner Dom, Humboldt-Box, Attrappe der Schinkelschen Bauakademie.

p. 89
The James-Simon-Gallery (Simon was an art patron before World War I), built by the architect David Chipperfield, was opened on July 12, 2019 and was the finishing touch for the external appearance of the Museumsinsel (museum island).

p. 107
The privately funded temporary Kunsthalle (art hall), which stood between September 2008 and August 2010, offered a place for both making and displaying contemporary international art in Berlin.

p. 118
Karl Friedrich Schinkel, the great Prussian architect and founder of Schinkel's Building Academy, is standing on the middle column in front of the pseudo-façade of his Academy, which was destroyed by bombings. The reconstruction is currently under debate.

p. 133
From left to right: Friedrichswerder Church, Berlin Cathedral, Humboldt-Box, pseudo-façade of the Schinkel Building Academy.

VITA | VITA

Tassilo Bonzel wurde in Olpe in Westfalen geboren und lebt in Fulda. Er fotografiert seit dem 8. Lebensjahr, beschäftigte sich Jahrzehnte als Kardiologe mit medizinischer Bildgebung und hat dabei gelernt, hinter die Bilder zu schauen. Seit 2009 widmet er sich Projekten der freien Fotografie. Seine Liebe zu Berlin begann mit dem Studium an der Freien Universität im Jahre 1963. Für das Projekt ‚Baustelle Berlin-Mitte' ist er seit 2007 regelmäßig mit dem Fahrrad im historischen Zentrum der Stadt unterwegs.

Einführung:
Ines Hahn lebt und arbeitet schon immer in Berlin. Sie studierte Theaterwissenschaften an der Humboldt-Universität zu Berlin, war zunächst wissenschaftliche Mitarbeiterin am Märkischen Museum und ist seit 2003 Kuratorin für Fotografie des Stadtmuseums Berlin.

Tassilo Bonzel was born in Olpe, Westfalia, and now lives in Fulda. He has been taking photographs since he got his first camera at the age of eight. Later he spent many decades in his career as a cardiologist working with medical images, which taught him to look beyond what is immediately visible. Since 2009 he has worked as an independent photographer on various projects. His love for Berlin began in 1963 when he was a medical student at the Free University. He began the project 'Building Berlin' in 2007, and since then has regularly used his bicycle for photographic tours of the city's historical center.

Ines Hahn has always lived and worked in Berlin. She studied drama at the Humboldt-University and was a research fellow at the Märkisches Museum, before in 2003 she was appointed curator for photography at the Berlin City Museum.

DANKSAGUNG | THANKS

Ich danke Peter Fauland, Fotograf, Berlin, für fototechnische Unterstützung; Dr. Katie Sutton, Canberra für fachkundige Hilfe bei der Übersetzung und meiner Tochter, der Filmwissenschaftlerin und Fotografin Dr. Katharina Bonzel, für ihren kritischen Blick und hilfreiche Kommentare; Frau Ines Hahn, Stadtmuseum Berlin, für die Einführung und Martin Düspohl, Kulturprojekte Berlin, für hilfreiche Anregungen. Nicht zuletzt danke ich Frau Margarita Licht vom Michael Imhof Verlag für das wunderschöne Layout und Dr. Michael Imhof für den Mut, dieses Buch zu publizieren.

Warm thanks to the following people for their assistance with various aspects of this project: photographer Peter Fauland, Berlin, for technical assistance; Katie Sutton, PhD, for assistance with the English translation and my daughter, screen studies scholar and photographer Katharina Bonzel, PhD (both Canberra) for her critical eye and constructive commentary; Ines Hahn, Berlin City Museum for the great introduction; Martin Düspohl, Kulturprojekte Berlin, for helpful stimulation; Margarita Licht, Michael Imhof publishing house, for the great layout and Dr. Michael Imhof for his courage, to publish this book.